East Meets West
Table Setting

East Meets West
Table Setting

Table Design and Food
By Kuwako Takahashi

Photography
By Hugo Steccati

SHUFUNOTOMO CO., LTD.

First printing, 1991

Photography by Hugo Steccati
English text supervised by Sally F. Sutherland
Book design and illustrations by Office 21

Published by Shufunotomo Co., Ltd.
2-9, Kanda Surugadai, Chiyoda-ku,
Tokyo, 101 Japan

Printed in Japan
ISBN4-07-975138-9

To all my Ikebana friends

Acknowledgments

My deepest appreciation goes to Hugo Steccati for his enthusiasm, expert photographs and his untiring tenacity. Without his ingenuity and vision, some of the scenes would not have been possible.

My heartiest thanks to Sally and Spence Sutherland for assisting us at the photo sessions. Their patient readiness in completing the project made the work so much easier. Also I am truly indebted to Sally for editing my English.

I count my blessings in having so many friends who opened their homes for the photographs. The varied atmosphere of these homes contributes a great deal to this book, and I am very grateful to all.

I would like to thank Shufunotomo Company for their trust in me in publishing this book. My special thanks go to editor Michiko Kinoshita, who is always a pleasure to work with.

Lastly I would like to thank my husband Yasundo for his support, my sister Hisako Yasuda, and my niece Mari Kohjima for having been my purveyors of hard-to-find items in Japan.

Preface

When we have guests we think about food, drink, and the setting. Food entails shopping and preparation. But choosing dishes for the table is a pure pleasure for me! It is like choosing a dress for my food. Then I choose placemats and napkins to enhance the dishes and a centerpiece that will incorporate all the colors, or at least something that relates to the tablewares. People notice the special attention given to the setting. It is a visual treat that embraces guests the minute they enter the room, starting conversation and multiplying the pleasures of a party.

It is fun to think of a special theme for a gathering and work toward it. If there is no particular theme, emphasize the season. Create a table that is visually cool in summer, warm in winter. Feature some flowers from your garden. You don't need an abundance of colorful flowers. Having a few flowers, simply arranged, makes a sophisticated table if the color scheme is carried out carefully.

A monochromatic setting is tranquil and soothing, but adding a contrasting color perks up a table, making it more vibrant. Using many bright colors creates an exciting table suitable for a festive occasion. But to avoid a jumbled look, add a neutral color as a binder, and proportion the colors to your liking.

To achieve an elegant and serene table, the best way is to determine the most important item on the table. If you want to use a certain dish, start your plan from it, expanding it to placemats, napkins, and centerpiece. If you decide to use a center runner such as an *obi*, repeat its colors on the table. Or if some artifact is used as a centerpiece, naturally you will emphasize it with harmonious or contrasting colors, and by linking it with some of the tableware. Many times you may have more objects you want to use in one setting. If they are not compatible, you should sacrifice one of them in order to create an uncluttered, serene table.

When a table is set with a harmonious plan, the table is like a musical composition. There is a phrase, some repetitions of the phrase, and the chords. The whole table, the tableware and centerpiece seem to be closely interwoven in a composition that radiates a charm of its own. You may have a beautiful dish, but if you don't have a setting to show it off, it is just a dish. A successful setting illustrates the beauty of the dishes and relates everything to the central theme.

I love dishes, but no one can collect an unlimited variety of them. What I like to do is use what I have in many different ways by changing accessories. One easy way is with napkins. By adapting *Origami* techniques, napkins can be folded into many shapes. At the end of this book, various instructions and diagrams are given. Most of them are simple yet very effective.

When choosing a basic set of dishes, my advice is to select the plainest, simplest dishes of good quality. This is not easy, because there are many attractive dishes with eye-catching designs available. Save these for your second purchase. Plain dishes center attention on the food placed on them like a picture, and I think this is the most important function of a dish. Plain dishes combine well with other dishes to create complex effects. Plain dishes adapt themselves like chameleons to any setting you create by simply changing placemats and napkins. My basic set is white porcelain with platinum rim. I bought them when we moved to Berkeley more than thirty years ago. Several years later I added another set of plain white dishes fluted like a chrysanthemum flower. These two sets can be combined with other bright dishes or lacquerwares. I still love using them so much that you will see them often in this book.

Next time you have company, just start planning a few days earlier. Think about what you can do for the table. Look around your house; you may find some artifact you have forgotten. Or you may find some interesting weed in your garden. Dream about the table and have fun setting it!

Kuwako Takahashi
Berkeley, California
Spring 1991

CONTENTS

Spring

Plum Blossom Time

Japanese plum blossom blooms as a harbinger of spring, permeating the air with its subtle fragrance. No wonder this was the most cherished flower of the Heian Period when *Tale of Genji* was written. This gorgeous palanquin of *Imari* ware reminded me of scenes from the scroll of *Tale of Genji* when Prince Genji visits a lover, and his palanquin awaits him outside. Pine and plum branches arranged on a black lacquer board with small rocks and sand create the scene. Napkins are folded like the love notes that were tied to flower branches and presented to lovers.

Imari ware seems to captivate Westerners with its warm colors and intricate designs! Here, the exquisite *Imari* plates are beautifully set off by the cinnabar placemats accented with blue napkins. The addition of western accessories such as antique silver candelabra and silver-rimmed glasses seems to enhance the glamorous feeling of this table.

Home of the late Mrs. Harlan Taylor
Menlo Park, California

Anniversary Table
for Two

Red and white flowering plum branches, white blossoms on the wall screen and red arranged in an elegant black lacquer container, seem to reach towards the table, blessing the happy couple.

The lovely Japanese fan spreading wide symbolizes future prosperity. The fan is repeated on the table as an auspicious theme. Both the antique, rust-colored small trays and black lacquer service trays are fan shaped, as are the decorative toothpicks used for appetizers. The antique container is adorned with fan patterns and the chopstick rests are small, closed fans. The napkins are tucked under the tray like half-opened fans and for a final touch, red and white miniature fans announce the occasion and the menu!

Home of Mrs. Fay Kramer
San Francisco, California

Impromptu Supper

At four o'clock the telephone rings announcing a sudden visit of an old friend. Of course we must get together. So the action starts. Some meat sauce is taken out of the freezer for defrosting. Salad is going to be mixed vegetables found in the refrigerator. A bottle of wine is placed in the refrigerator. What about the table? Well, the tomato meat sauce is red, and so are apples and cranberries I happen to have. So the key color is red, and nothing complements it better than black dishes! I also found red paper placements and napkins, left over from Valentine Day. Black Japanese burnt cedar trays for hot towels are just right for the baguettes.

I looked around the kitchen for some gadgets that would make an interesting, whimsical centerpiece, and I decided on wire whisks. I propped them up with a tumbler. As for flowers, I rolled up strips of red tissue paper and tied them on wire stems. Cranberries were spread to form a base. In keeping with the improvisation, I cored a couple of red apples to use as the candlesticks. As a final touch, I added some dry caspia as a softener. How do you like it? We had a great time!

Takahashi residence
Berkeley, California

Homage to Mr. Sofu Teshigahara

This table is dedicated to the late Mr. Sofu Teshigahara, the legendary headmaster of Sogetsu School of Ikebana whose calligraphy graces the wall. He was not only a genius in ikebana, revitalizing this century-old Japanese art, but also a superb artist in many other fields. This dramatic calligraphy, *Nichirin*, meaning great sun, was done for a demonstration in San Francisco in 1961. I still remember his spectacular finish by throwing a big brush right into the center of the circle at the left, making a splashy blob to complete the character for sun!

One of his favorite foods was *sushi* which is arranged on a bright orange platter which was given to me by a friend and collaborator on this book. I thought the platter looked just like a sun, and perfect for this table. The center runner has another dramatic calligraphy—it is an enlarged print of the *Jyoruri* Book with its typical bold strokes. *Jyoruri* is one of the chanting accompaniments to Kabuki plays, therefore it is right at home with *sushi* which was developed in Tokyo in the 19th century by the common people who patronized Kabuki theater.

The fan-shaped varnished bamboo dishes also have *Jyoruri* print. The soup bowls, the dishes for soy sauce, the chopsticks and the fanshaped dishes are all cinnabar color. To set off this color, double-faced mats, black with cinnabar, are folded diagonally showing the black side under the dish. The napkins are red and white *kanoko* print, one of the traditional patterns often seen in Kabuki costumes. A red-framed, antique hand lantern is a final touch for this table of calligraphy and Kabuki theme.

Takahashi residence
Berkeley, California

Dancing Butterflies

Phalaenopsis is commonly called butterfly orchid. Pink flowers clustered on a slender stem do look like flying butterflies! To emphasize the airiness, the orchid spray is arranged in a crystal vase placed on a free-form mirror base. The arrangement is devoid of any greens, making it more fantasy-like with some misty gypsophila. The white butterflies scattered on the mirror are Japanese chopstick rests but also very useful as decoration. The glass marbles, looking like dew drops, add sparkle. Pink, tapered candles are in star-like, transparent candlesticks. Pink napkins are folded into sunbursts making the table really glamorous! When using a sweet color like pink, one must be cautious not to go overboard. Here, to balance the pink, cool, silver-rimmed white plates and white and silver woven placemats are used, making a romantic table elegant enough for an engagement dinner.

Takahashi residence
Berkeley, California

Camellia Table

My camellia starts to bloom in January and continues to spring. I just love the simple flower with its distinct stamen. For an early spring luncheon, camellias are featured with bamboo in the background arrangement and in the centerpiece. The centerpiece is a composition of a bamboo structure which serves as a container for camellias and green bamboo candles. Instead of dishes, I used bamboo baskets with handles for serving *tempura*. The baskets are a common shape like the ones used on an outing to collect young greens, a nostalgic reminiscence of bygone days. The paper placemats are light green, the color of spring fields. The camellia dishes for dipping sauce are pink, and so is the paper lining of the baskets. The placemats and basket linings were cut from paper bought at an art supply store. Red lacquer chopsticks match the color of the red camellia and they rest on green holders shaped like fern shoots, another reminder of spring fields.

Takahashi residence
Berkeley, California

Doll Festival

When March comes along with bright sunshine, it is time for the Doll Festival—a custom that has been carried from generation to generation in Japan. Families with daughters celebrate on March third by displaying a set of dolls depicting the royal court of the Heian Period.

This elegant dining room, paneled with a beautiful gold screen with a green pine tree, is a perfect foil for this festival. The emperor and empress sit in front of the gold screen, flanked by screens of forsythia which is bright yellow like spring sunshine. With this background, gold is the natural choice for this table and metallic gold fabric is used for the center runner. On it stands a bronze gourd, with its gracefully sprawling orange cord, holding a branch of pink peach blossom, a flower essential for this festival! More branches of pink and white peach blossom are elegantly packed in gold and orange paper folded in a classic way. Two pairs of triangular oil lamps suggest two pairs of dolls. On gold lacquered service plates, the napkins are folded like *hina* dolls with a red napkin with red camellia as an empress and a green napkin with white tulip as an emperor. All hold fan-shaped name cards.

Dining room of Mr. & Mrs. Martin Gordon
Corte Madera, California

Drop In For a Drink!

"Aren't they beautiful!" The ladies standing in the flowing robes, looking outside, seem to be admiring the cherry blossoms in the garden. Perhaps the ladies and the noblemen inside may be contemplating their poems. The lovely *Tale of Genji* screen evokes the joy of life.

The vermilion silk brocade *obi* repeats the color of the robes and radiates the elegant ambiance of the screen to the table. The color is further intensified by the lacquer ware—a covered bowl for salad, the tray holding rolled sandwiches, and the fluted dishes. Green maple dishes and plum-shaped bowls for nuts repeat the design of the *obi*. Another unusual antique piece here is the bronze candlestick—a pair of graceful cranes holds gold candles. The napkins are handkerchieves with *Tale of Genji* pictures.

Home of Mr. & Mrs. Kent Atwater
Hillsborough, California

Cherry Blossom Viewing Picnic

The anxiously awaited date comes! The weather is fine and the cherry blossoms are at their prime. Nothing compares to the ethereal beauty of the pink cloud against the blue sky! It is an exhilarating experience, basking in the warm sun and sharing the joy with your friends.

As depicted in many antique screens and pictures, cherry blossom viewing has been a major event in the life of Japanese people for many centuries. The springtime outing has become such a ritual that the Japanese designed a special lunch box to carry food for the picnic. It is called *Hanami Jyu*, lunch boxes for cherry blossom viewing. The *Hanami Jyu* shown here is of the late 19th century and is adorned with a flowering cherry tree. Many sets are designed with family crests. Four stacked boxes for food, two pewter *sake* jugs that stand on a box containing five small dishes, another box for wooden eating forks, and a tray with a *sake* cup—all go into a frame with a handle, forming a compact carrying case. It is a fine example

of the Japanese genius for combining the ultimate utility with beauty!

A low table is covered with red felt. Traditionally the cloth was spread on the ground for people and food, but for more comfortable seating, I arranged black lacquer stools topped with round cushions of bamboo shoot husks. The stools are part of a lacquer set used for outdoor tea ceremony. When the food is placed on the table, it becomes quite beautiful, framed by the bright orange-red background, as if being lighted on a stage.

Another custom traditionally observed with the viewing is poetry making and writing. Poems of thirty-one syllables (*Waka*) or seventeen syllables (*Haiku*) are written on long strips of colored paper and hung on the branches of cherry trees. Then, one indulges in drinking and eating to one's heart's content while savoring the heavenly day!

Garden of Mr. & Mrs. George Morishige
Berkeley, California

31

Dessert on Skewers
(See page 30.)

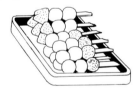

Fruit Version
Strawberry, banana and
green grapes on
skewers, just like the
traditional dumplings.

"Hanami Dango"
Cherry Blossom Viewing
Dumplings
Traditional sweets made in
pink, white and
green colors on bamboo
skewers.

Cherry Blossom Viewing Picnic

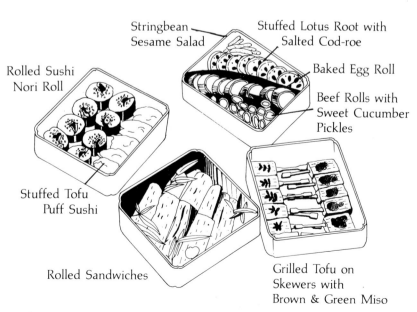

Stringbean
Sesame Salad

Stuffed Lotus Root with
Salted Cod-roe

Baked Egg Roll

Rolled Sushi
Nori Roll

Beef Rolls with
Sweet Cucumber
Pickles

Stuffed Tofu
Puff Sushi

Rolled Sandwiches

Grilled Tofu on
Skewers with
Brown & Green Miso

In the lacquer box at the left, clockwise from the left front: pink cherry blossom rice molded in the shape of a cherry blossom petal; baked tofu loaf and mustard green pickles; grated daikon salad topped with red caviar and ginger needles in a cherry blossom flower bowl; boiled prawn, quail's egg and cucumber on a bamboo skewer; simmered bamboo shoot and snow peas.

On the tray at the right, a black lacquer bowl has a clear soup with boiled daikon slice and cherry blossom petals scattered on. On a small square paper sits a sake cup.

Indoor Cherry Blossom Viewing

In Japan, cherry blossom viewing is almost a national obsession. The date of blossom time is announced in newspapers and people gather around the flowering trees to drink, eat, sing and have a good time! If you have neither time nor a garden to visit, you can still enjoy cherry blossoms by arranging a branch on a table.

Here is an indoor party with Japanese boxed lunches. Like a *Haiku* poem, the scene on the lacquer tray has everything: a cherry tree in full bloom, scattering petals on a stream; a miniature hand lantern suggesting blossoms viewed in the evening! The square, lacquered *Shokado* lunch box is as practical as it is pretty. The lid, when opened and placed upside down, becomes a tray for a soup bowl, *sake* cup and chopsticks. For Japanese meals, the dishes are chosen with great care. Hosts or chefs enjoy sending unspoken messages about the season or occasion through the selection of dishes used or the way food is served. Here, the graceful *sake* pitcher, *sake* cups, and cherry blossom-shaped bowls are all Hagi ware with a hazy pink-beige tone similar to cherry blossoms. The pink-colored rice is molded into the shape of a cherry petal, as is the chopstick rest. Clear soup with a round daikon slice has cherry blossom petals floating in it, suggesting a full moon with cherry blossoms!

Japanese room of Mr. & Mrs. George Morishige Berkeley, California

Table with Square Fans

A handsome, redwood-paneled dining room makes a perfect setting for this table featuring tanned, square fans. Fans are usually associated with summer, but this special tanned fan is treated with the astringent juice of persimmon for strength and was a year-round kitchen tool. It was indispensable for starting a fire to cook on. When it was torn, it was patched with any paper, whether a calligraphy practice paper or an old *Jyoruri* Book, resulting in an interesting collage. The fans used here are new, but simulate the effect. Tan linen napkins folded into squares are tucked under the fan, repeating the form. The burnt cedar round dishes are black, the color of the calligraphy, and so are the chopsticks. The unusual slant-cut *sake* cups and the chopstick rests are both varnished bamboo. The vase is an old *Binbo Dokkuri*, poorman's *sake* jug. It is so called because it bore the *sake* store's name and was given away to customers who bought *sake* by the jugful. The brown kiwi vines arranged in the jug seem to extend the calligraphy with an airy flourish. The spray of yellow Oncydium orchid brightens up this table of earthy tones, and dark brown lotus seedpods add some weight to the airy centerpiece. The interesting candle holders of dark wood are parts of old spools. The brown table runner with a white stripe is a narrow woven *obi* for an everyday kimono.

Thus everything on this table relates to the everyday life of common people of generations ago in Japan. The objects have a subtle, subdued serenity and an undeniable charm which might be described as being *shibui*. While not dramatic, this table has a soothing calmness.

Home of Mrs. Pearl Kimura
Berkeley, California

Summer

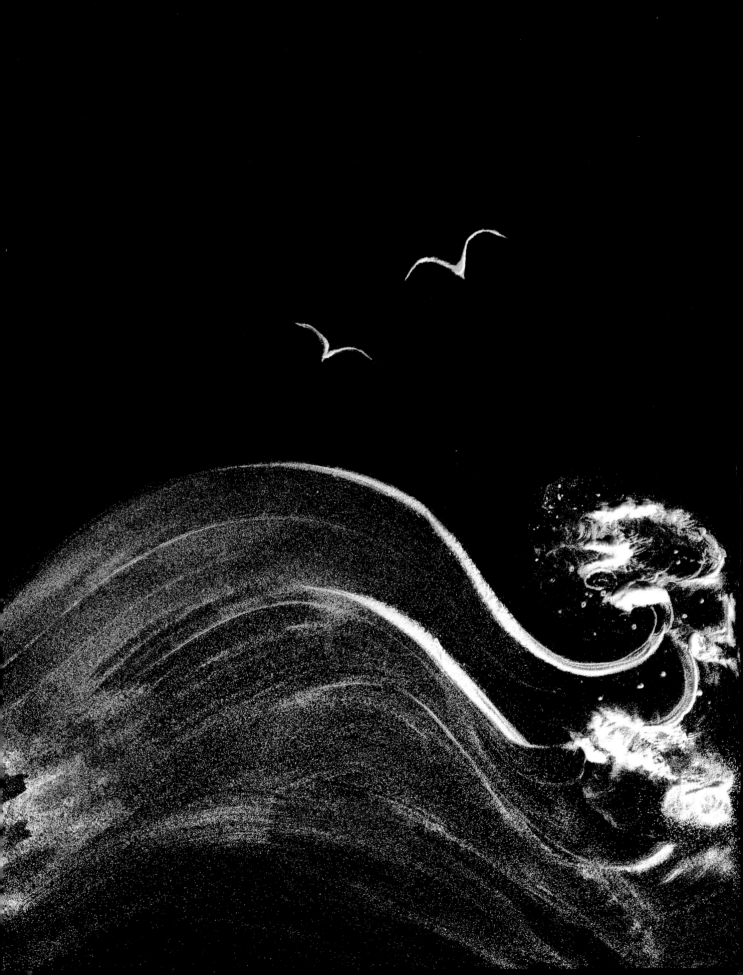

Iris Day in May

On the fifth of May Japanese families with boys celebrate their good fortune by hoisting fish kites and displaying helmet, horse and warrior dolls, repeating the custom dating back to feudal times. The flower symbolizing this festival is Japanese iris, and the festival is called Iris Day or May Festival. Some westerners refer to it as Boy's Day. In keeping with the spirit of this festival, I planned a table that is simple and masculine.

Using gold-rimmed black lacquer containers, I arranged iris as though growing in a pond, bringing part of the iris pond to the table as the centerpiece. Using two strips of wood which normally are used as a base for arrangements, and some twigs, I constructed a raised walk through the iris pond like those seen in Ogata Korin's iris screen, and placed it between the two iris groups. Black pebbles scattered around make it look more like a garden.

The placemats are woven silk from Thailand in warm, deep brown. Instead of dishes, I chose rectangular varnished boards of natural wood on which I placed something special for this day. The white paper is ordinary typewriting paper folded to look like a helmet. With dewy iris blades tucked in, an unmistakable touch for Iris Day is added. The first course appetizers placed on the paper are fried shrimp in an edible basket of deep-fried, woven seaweed and boiled fava beans. Green bamboo *sake* cups and green bamboo chopsticks complete the verdant mood of this setting. The chopsticks are placed vertically on the horizontal stripes of the napkins to emphase the contrast, and rest on wooden holders shaped like arrowheads, very suitable for this festival.

Home of Mrs. Pearl Kimura
Berkeley, California

Imari and Czechoslovakian Glass

A collection of *Imari* ware and antique, handblown glass inspired me to compose this table. When they were placed side by side, I was surprised how well they complemented each other. They have affinities in color and design in spite of their differences in source and material.

This *Imari* ware has strong blue in various shades, an accent of dark red, and a bit of green on white. To bring them out, I made plain placemats and napkins in medium blue and light blue. A magenta cymbidium orchid was placed on each napkin, to repeat the dark red of the *Imari*. The setting is predominantly blue, so to balance this, the centerpiece was made more white

and magenta with a touch of blue-purple wild iris. Fortunately an ikebana friend had given me this magenta-colored orchid which was just right with the *Imari* red, and the fluffy white flowers used here were an unexpected find in the parking lot of a store we stopped by that morning. It is the flower of an unknown weed. The vase used here is an antique bronze of lotus leaves and stems which seems to lift the arrangement. With the line of orchid leaves, the arrangement creates an air of flowing onto the silver and navy blue brocade *obi*.

Home of Mr. & Mrs. Kent Atwater
Hillsborough, California

A Birthday Party

A child's birthday party is always fun to plan because it is one of the happiest occasions in any family. It should be colorful and carefree.

At a party supply store I found these paper hats with polka dots in bright colors, just like balloons. To complement the hats, I bought paper plates and napkins in several bright colors, and plastic flatware and paper cups in red and yellow.

A peach-colored tablecloth made a warm background for all the wild colors. Napkins were folded like *origami* lotus flowers and placed on the plates, holding the hats or any favors you might have.

The birthday cake was decorated like a drum, a circus drum to go with a clown that is hanging from a balloon. I mobilized my Japanese folk toys, birds, dogs, horses, oxen, etc. to circle around the cake like a circus ring. The colorful cat-like animal in the back is actually a papier-mache dog which is given to newborn babies with a wish for their healthy growth. So here are many symbols wishing health and happiness to the lucky child!

Home of Mr. & Mrs. Iain Finnie
Berkeley, California

Table with Wisteria Obi

Using *obi* on tables was an astounding revelation to the Japanese! But they do add glamour to a table. A splendid wedding *obi* brightens up a table on a special occasion, and quiet, old-fashioned ones create a serene elegance for any table.

This silver *obi* with wisteria and iris is a portion of a *maru Obi*, a formal *obi* for full-dress kimono, with flowers of all seasons hand-painted all over.

At a department store in Tokyo I found these lavender placemats of woven hemp and crinkly, silk-like polyester napkins in a lighter shade with a pine, bamboo and plum motif scattered in white. They enhance the *obi* by bringing out the color and contrast in texture. For the dishes, I used the salad plate of my platinum-rimmed dinner set and shallow celadon bowls. The celadon seems to perk up the table by picking up the color of wisteria and iris leaves.

The centerpiece is very simple because the *obi* is the major factor on this table. A single Japanese iris of deep lavender is arranged with leaves in an off-white Sogetsu vase. The two-paneled silver screen painted with wild chrysanthemums, a work of my late father-in-law, makes a pleasant backdrop.

Takahashi residence
Berkeley, California

48

A Picnic in Green Shade

Set on a bamboo-floored balcony and flanked by graceful black bamboo, this table is designed to enhance the ambiance by using natural materials like bamboo containers and aralia or fatsia japonica leaves. There is also a hidden magic in the paper lunch package.

Sake cups and a pitcher are made of green bamboo; a couple of giant bamboo sections hold vegetable sticks and cherries; another slant-cut bamboo container—from *Take Dera* or Bamboo Temple outside Tokyo—holds skewered food for barbecue. Hot towels are on small bamboo trays and iced tea glasses are in bamboo baskets usually used for the towels. Dramatic leaves of aralia are placed like trays or doilies.

The neat square package unfolds to reveal many secrets. It first opens to a four-pointed star holding a couple of light and dark sandwiches. Then pulling out the bottom opens up another layer containing pound-cake slices and chocolate! These are made from two sheets of colored paper bought from an art supply store. It is fun to make these.

The napkins are made from Japanese cotton towels with white pine needles on dark green. The dainty barbecue on the table comes from the Hida region in Japan and is called *Hida Konro*.

At the garden of Mr. & Mrs. John Planting
Palo Alto, California

Summer Lunch by a Pond

At an old pond,
  A frog jumps in,
    Making a splashy sound of water.

This famous *haiku* by Basho is visualized on this table. On the oval black lacquer board, three circles with different diameters are made by placing round lids of various sizes and sifting fine white sand or super-fine sugar over the edge. A ceramic frog in the center of the circles with several ceramic lily pads make the board seem like a pond. Black pebbles mark the shoreline where several reeds and round leaves of wild ginger or Asarum Caudatum in a water-holding, needlepoint holder add to the feeling of the waterside marsh. A lily pad with a stem is a souvenir ash tray from the Lafcadio Hearn Museum in Matsue, Japan.

White, Japanese fan-shaped porcelain dishes with green maple leaves look nice on this green table and are large enough for a salad or a first course. Small maple leaf dishes in deep green continue the maple theme and are lovely for small rolls. Dainty Japanese glasses are placed on fresh maple leaves. Bamboo-handled flatware rest on chopstick holders of green water-plant leaves.

Home of Mr. & Mrs. George Morishige
Berkeley, California

Brunch Table with Goldfish

Why not have some goldfish swimming on a table when the temperature is high and everybody longs for cool water!

This sunny terrace with lush green maples, azalea bushes and a turquoise pool behind makes an ideal place for this table. The glass table top has a surface similar to that of water under light wind. With a pair of goldfish in a clear bowl placed on water lily pads, the table assumes the look of a pond. The yellow, ceramic lily pad dishes not only keep the theme but also add the sunny brightness of a summer morning. Red napkins are folded like fish, and when they are placed, slightly curled, on the dish, the "fish" appear to swim.

A cool breeze makes a glass windbell ring, and with the tempting aroma of fragrant coffee and fresh croissants in a yellow napkin lotus flower, the table invites you for a leisurely brunch to start a pleasant day!

In the garden of Mr. & Mrs. Norman Cima
Menlo Park, California

Fourth of July

Coming at the height of summer, July fourth with its parades and fireworks evokes exultation. So on this table, using the traditional, patriotic colors of red, white, and blue, I tried to express the feeling of jubilation.

The centerpiece, flanked by blue candles in star-shaped candlesticks, consists of white hydrangea, lace flowers, gypsophila, tropicana roses, blue campanulas and bachelor's buttons. It looks like fireworks exploding to the sky!

Red Thai placemats make brilliant backgrounds for the white, fluted plates. Blue napkins folded into lotus flowers encase white, flower-shaped bowls. Jewel-like cherry tomatoes and blueberries, marinated in dressing and well chilled, make a wonderfully refreshing start for a dinner as well as adding a crowning visual touch to this table.

To show what a dramatic variation can be made by a single change, the same table was photographed again using white placemats. Everything else remains the same, but the difference is spectacular! With more white, the table is serene and more formal compared to the jubilant red table.

Takahashi residence
Berkeley, California

Lunch on a Sausalito Hillside

The view from this balcony is breathtaking! Sitting on a hillside above the town of Sausalito, surrounded by old live oak trees, the balcony offers a panorama of green hills, an island on the blue, shimmering bay that extends to the purple hills of the East Bay. The air is crystal clear. It is warm, yet cool enough to enjoy the July sun.

The color for this table is yellow gold, the color of the California sun. The centerpiece is edible. The beautiful vegetables from the summer abundance: cauliflower, carrots, cucumbers, radishes, red and yellow cherry tomatoes, on skewers and stuck into a head of cabbage, brighten the table like a bouquet. They are also delicious eaten with dipping sauces. Two grapefruits covered with daisies emphasize the gold and white and assume the position of centerpieces when the vegetables are finished and removed.

The plates are plain white porcelain on which yellow napkins shaped into pouches are placed. The flatware in the pouches keeps napkins from flying away.

Balcony of Mr. & Mrs. Spence Sutherland
Sausalito, California

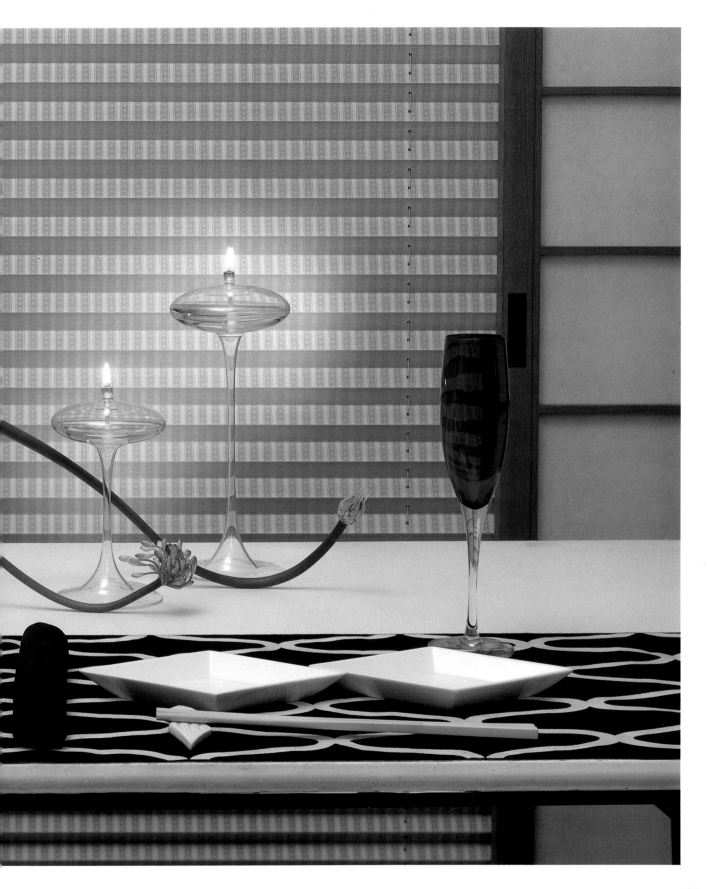

Yukata Table

Yukata is cotton cloth worn as summer kimono in Japan. The color is predominantly white with navy blue, the most soothing color combination in the humid, hot climate. Each year textile makers present new designs. However, many century-old, classic patterns remain popular. This streamlined, white net design on navy blue is a good example of classic designs with clear-cut simplicity that never lose their appeal. Placed on a white table, it is strikingly contemporary!

For a Japanese setting, I chose plain white porcelain dishes in diamond shape. Two of them are placed side by side, one for an endive leaf with cottage cheese and salted fish roe, the other for a striped *sushi* of smoked salmon and cucumber. White chopsticks rest on white ceramic holders that repeat diamond shapes. Bright blue Italian glasses in elongaged forms echo the flowing line of the design which is further dramatized by the two marvelously cursive lines of the agapanthus stems given to me by an ikebana friend. The arrangement in a round, compact vase with a couple of cool caladium leaves and mass of purple agapanthus flowers seems to fly on the table. Two dome-shaped oil lamps on gracefully stretched stands cast a soft glow.

For a western setting, navy blue napkins folded into roses are placed on plain white plates, creating a theme of round forms which is repeated with the wine glasses and in the centerpiece composition. On the base of blue pebbles in sweeping form, three ball-shaped oil lamps and a couple of white hydrangea flowers nestle together. The blue pebbles are from an aquarium supply store.

Home of Mr. & Mrs. George Morishige
Berkeley, California

The Call of the Sea

Everything on this table relates to the sea, because it is set in the garden of a friend who used to be an ardent fisherman.

The sand-colored tablecloth is covered with black, polyethylene net suggesting a fishnet on a beach. On a black lacquer board, grilled fish, the catch of the day, are swimming on a dashing breaker made with salt. Fresh pickled ginger, the garnish to the fish, is served on bamboo leaf boats. Napkins folded like old Japanese fishing boats sit on square, *tenmoku*-glazed plates. Black lacquer chopsticks rest on river trout holders. Boiled fresh soy beans, a favorite Japanese appetizer in summer, are in miniature fish baskets. The salad of vegetables and seaweed is served in a giant scallop shell. Candles are in shells and a rock. A pair of iron crabs seem to be enjoying an evening stroll on a beach scattered with shells and corals.

In the garden of Mrs. Pearl Kimura
Berkeley, California

68

Fantasy in Glass

Glass ware in any form holds unfailing fascination for me. In various lights and backgrounds, it unfolds its magical charms.

The starting point for this table was the marriage of American rain glass plates with Japanese soup bowls. When I saw these bowls in Tokyo, instantly I recalled the plates and to my pleasure, the pairing was perfect. Periwinkle, cool color of water and sky, is used as the basic color to bring out the transparency of the glass. To add to this combination, we settled on cut glass for wine. Wonderful rings of transparent acrylic circle the periwinkle napkins. Japanese porcelain bowls were added because of their interesting shape and the matching color.

The centerpiece consists of glass in various forms. Water-filled cylinders in several heights, ball-shaped oil lamps and iridescent marbles are spread on a free-form mirror to heighten the magic of light and crystal! Hydrangeas in various shades of blue to pink arranged in masses add the color and textural interest to the centerpiece, and extend the color theme to the buffet in back. All the hydrangea leaves are removed to keep the world of fantasy.

Home of Mr. & Mrs. Norman Cima
Menlo Park, California

Summer Breeze

The blue California native morning glory is arranged on the wall in an antique basket. The table is set with bamboo placemats similar to the bamboo shade. The appetizer trays are varnished wood round fans from Kyoto. The dainty porcelain morning glory flower bowls arranged on the fan with the vines of morning glory make an alluring presentation for summer! The small bowls contain grated cucumber and red caviar. Other appetizers are *daikon* sticks rolled with prosciutto and Provolone cheese rolled with *nori*. The unvarnished chopsticks with tapered ends are used for formal Japanese dinners. Valuing unvarnished wood over colorful lacquer comes from the Shinto ceremony which uses unvarnished, virgin wood for the service ware. The chopstick rests are deep blue, glass eggplants, and this blue is repeated in the white *Yukata* cloth napkins with iris and stream pattern. The contemporary *sake* set of cracked-ice glass adds a welcome coolness to the table and is placed on square-cut, light green Japanese paper with a summer grass motif.

   The coolest centerpiece you can arrange is water. Here, I am using a black lacquer container, one of Mr. Sofu Teshigahara's design. The L-shaped shallow container is filled with water, and I arranged variegated miscanthus—Japanese pampas grass—fern, and round leaves of wild ginger, some of them floated like lily pads. All green and nothing but grasses. The final touch is lily pad candles that float in the water!

Takahashi residence
Berkeley, California

Summer Festival

On the evening of July 7, the legend of *Tanabata*, the Star Festival, says a cowherd star and a weaver star rendezvous once a year on the Milky Way, called the River of Heaven. It began as a romantic festival, but later it also became a festival of arts and crafts. Children are encouraged to do calligraphy of poems or wishes on strips of colored paper. They also make rainbow-colored streamers reflecting the weaver's yarns, and paper fishnets referring to the River of Heaven. Freshly cut bamboo decorated with these is as essential to this festival as a Christmas tree is to Christmas.

On a balcony overlooking the San Francisco Bay, facing the Golden Gate Bridge, a table is set with a navy blue cloth to intensify the evening atmosphere. A couple of golden bamboo adorned with colorful streamers and paper strips stand against the evening sky's lingering glow.

I made the lantern with wood and paper and wrote "Summer Festival" in Japanese calligraphy. Backed by the bamboo it is the centerpiece for this table. On summer evenings, lantern light always heightens the excitement. A red round fan with a black character for "festival", a ceremonial *sake* keg of varnished wood with an orange accent and a couple of festival *happi* coats made from folded Japanese towels are placed around the table as mementoes of summer festivals.

Brown lacquer, round fan-shaped service plates are perfect for this table, setting off the cobalt blue glass plates which are matched in color by the tall tumblers. The white and navy napkin is the typical *Yukata* cloth used for the uniformal festival kimono. The miniature blue *happi* coat with a white family crest placed on the napkin is a chopstick holder. A bamboo twig with colored paper adorns the square bamboo basket with crossed handles. The basket is modeled after a primitive fishing tool linking it symbolically to the River of Heaven. For the western setting, it is intended to serve as a bread plate.

For the Japanese setting, the baskets are used to serve some fried prawns, and the blue glass plates are replaced by brown lacquer, pail-shaped lunch boxes which are a very suitable choice because they relate to water. As the pails are identical in color with the service plates, folded napkins are placed between them. The handle of the pail is formed by the chopsticks inserted through the holes of the two sides.

What kind of treat would you expect in such a box? Here, it is barbecued eel on rice, which is perhaps the most popular summer food in Japan. Enjoy your dinner and let us make a toast to the beautiful summer evening. *Kanpai!*

Balcony of Mr. & Mrs. Iain Finnie
Berkeley, California

Fall

Milk Cartons on the Table?

Why not? After all, milk is a staple food in most households and its carton is a throwaway, so let's use the cartons. They are waterproof, easy to cut and glue together. A few years ago, I started to experiment making containers out of cartons. The hardest part is the painting, since several coats of spray paint are needed. For cutting, insert a block of wood and use a sharp-pointed knife. Cartons are a wonderful material to use for the study of creative forms.

Here is a composition made of five quart-sized cartons painted vermillion, shocking pink, fresh green and navy blue. The forms are blocks and cartwheel halves. Circular forms are repeated in wired equisetums, one of them starting from a fresh green ball of Granny Smith apple. The cartwheel shape is completed in the sunflower which is the focal point, and repeated in daisies stuck into the ends of equisetums. Surrounding this colorful centerpiece, yellow plastic plates and mugs accented by vermillion napkins make a delightfully bright table to start a day!

Home of Mr. & Mrs. John Cardoza
Berkeley, California

Harvest Table

In early fall, we are blessed with an abundance of fruits and vegetables that are as good to look at as to eat!

On the rosewood table, a couple of melons, Cranshaw and Casaba, are arranged on a split-bamboo runner, half-draped by a pumpkin vine with lush green foliage and yellow flowers. Slender Japanese cucumbers, eggplants, and golden squashes nestle under the foliage, creating a colorful composition.

A lifelike cricket is inspecting the melon. The Japanese enjoy the chirping of crickets so much that they are sold in small cages. A boat-shaped bamboo cage is placed in the back, as the cricket's house. The yellow onions in front are salt and pepper shakers.

The service trays are Japanese cedar from Akita. Green pumpkin leaves and bright yellow dishes stand out on the dark trays and highlight the glass compotes of chilled custard soup, *Hiyashi Chawanmushi*, garnished with edible yellow and orange nasturtium flowers. Brown napkins in brown cord rings keep low profiles beside the trays. In this beige-toned dining room with its screen of subdued hues and a handsome Chinese cabinet, the still life of the centerpiece and the flowery food on the trays seem to be vividly alive!

Home of Mr. & Mrs. John Cardoza
Berkeley, California

Moon Viewing

Moonlight seems to have a mystical power, casting a spell over people, making them wander into a strange land, away from the mundane world, and face the universe with its eternity. One realizes the insignificance and briefness of one's being; one thinks of past and future, of people far away and gone! Probably that is why the Japanese have been moon viewing for a thousand years.

We tried to create the scene here. A bright full moon is rising in the sky, casting the silhouettes of *Susuki*, Japanese pampas grass, on a *shoji* screen. *Susuki* is always associated with moon viewing.

On the table, *Susuki* is arranged tall, as it grows in the fields. The black vase symbolizes a full moon with its round window. The placemats, double-faced with tea green and yellow green, are folded like two hills from which the moon rises. The plates are crescents of translucent glass, a contemporary Japanese craft. Napkins are Japanese *Kaishi*, bosom paper, with a design of autumn grasses, tucked into the placemats. The *sake* set is of cracked-ice glass.

What kind of food to serve on such a dish? Any dainty hors d'œuvres would be nice. Here, a dessert is shown, a mousse of green tea and caramel cut into crescent moons.

Takahashi residence
Berkeley, California

A Folkcraft Table

This is a table using folkcraft items—humble objects made by simple people for their own use. The colors are sombre—black, gray, natural tan to dark brown, and dark blues.

The dominant piece is an iron hot pot with a burnt cedar lid with vivid grains. To set it off an indigo-dyed cotton cloth with circular motifs is used. The cauldron-shaped casseroles are the containers of a popular lunch *Kamameshi*, or cauldron rice, sold at Yokogawa railway station. Since white stands out on the indigo blue, white dishes of interesting shapes are used. Hexagonal dishes hold scallop-shell and bamboo spoons which are useful for lifting food from the hot pot. Sparrow dishes are for some sauce or condiments. Chopstick rests are water birds and the

stemware is Mexican blue glass. White kitchen towels with Japanese alphabet in navy blue are used as napkins.

The iron kettle is typical cast ironwork from the Nanbu area in northern Japan. Serene white Japanese bellflowers and caladium leaves are arranged in the kettle, adding a fresh touch. The pair of cute white porcelain bunnies from Germany huddle together, completing the accent of white on this table. On the windowsill stand three *Kokeshi* dolls in black on natural wood.

There is no primadonna on this table. Everything is subdued and austere and yet there is an appealing, refreshing quality!

Home of Mr. & Mrs. Spence Sutherland
Sausalito, California

Black and Gold Elegance

This off-white room, with deep beige carpet and a sofa backed by an antique screen with monochromatic, sumi-ink painting forms an ideal setting for a coffee table setting which was inspired by this exquisite black lacquer box with gold designs. The black and gold theme is splendidly carried out by a black *obi* with gold chrysanthemums.

Black lacquered small dishes with gold designs, each telling different stories from famous Noh plays with some related symbolic objects, are beside the box. There also are several varnished fan dishes in gold, mustard and gray.

On a raised tray at the left, a beach scene is made with a couple of black rocks. Nuts form the beach where treasure bags of yellow tomatoes with black caviar are laid, and cucumber boats with shrimp sails are in the bay. Nearby, an antique crane holds a candle.

Beige napkins are neatly lined up in front, overlapping each other. An array of off-white porcelain tea cups with equisetums in black with gold are for drinks. A pair of gorgeous black lacquer, antique candlesticks with beige candles tie the table to the screen. There is nothing dramatic in this setting, yet there is a subtle sophistication and elegance.

Home of Mr. & Mrs. Norman Cima
Menlo Park, California

89

Blue Bellflowers by a Stream

Japanese bellflowers are so alluring in their simplicity. Ever since I found these striking blue bowls in Japan, I wanted to do a table featuring them.

Here they are combined with an old *obi* with the design of bellflowers, wild pink, and Japanese pampas grass by a stream. It also shows bamboo baskets which were formerly used for the embankment of a river and still often appear in paintings. The motif is recreated on the table. The stream is made by a sand painting technique of sifting fine sand, and then moving a notched feather on the sand, making the flowing lines. The stream appears often in this book because it can be seen from both sides without distortion. Blue bellflowers are arranged in a container resembling the river embankment baskets, with variegated Japanese pampas grass and parsley flowers in a naturally growing fashion.

Gray Shino ware pottery dishes with brush marks are slightly darker gray than the *obi*. Napkins of lighter gray are folded into squares and placed on the dishes, beautifully setting off the blue bowls. Blue candles matching the bowls stand in black iron candlestands. Blue wine glasses are Mexican.

Flatware with bamboo-shaped handles are placed as the final touch to this Western setting using Japanese dishes and bowls.

Takahashi residence
Berkeley, California

The Night of Halloween

"In the darkness of a moonless night,
  When the bats fly around in the turbulent wind,
And a witch rides skyward and high,
  There is a gathering of a monstrous kind,
Pumpkin heads, screaming, grimacing
                                    or laughing at the fright.
A black cat comes alive with a fearless glare!"

The pumpkins are set on the table and surrounded by red lentil beans, walnuts in their shells, and dried corn with husks. The orange, pumpkin-shaped place-mats are cut from paper from an art supply store and folded to make pockets to hold Halloween gimmicks. The witch hats sitting on the black, *tenmoku*-glazed plates are quite easy to make from starched napkins. Stemware is pitch black glass, and so is the plastic flatware.

Takahashi residence
Berkeley, California

93

California Sun and Wine

Out on a terrace flooded by golden sunshine, a glass-topped table is set. White wrought iron chairs have the interesting design of bamboo culm, inspiring me to make a runner and placemats from an inexpensive, woven bamboo panel.

The sunflower which rises from the colored grape vine and white, peeled curly willow arrangement, symbolizes the California sun! The ever-bright, golden sun nurtures grapes which produce California wine. The wine, held high by the wrought iron grapevine of this unusual wine dispenser from Germany, sparkles like a jewel.

The table is set for wine and cheese. The square natural and black trays, *Hassun*, are normally used for serving appetizers at a Japanese dinner, but here they are used as service trays, setting off these rectangular glass dishes with wavy line designs. Black lacquer soup bowls, with a grape leaf motif in gold, hold fruits. The flatware is ebony-handled. Three kinds of cheese are on a square wooden tray lined with colorful grape leaves, and baguette slices are in a natural bamboo container. The beige napkins have my *haiku* written in Japanese.

"Ohgon no hikari no tsuyu ka? Umashi sake!"
Dewdrops of the golden sunshine?
The luscious, mellow wine!

Home of Mr. & Mrs. John Cardoza
Berkeley, California

Chrysanthemum Buffet

For a large party, buffet style is a solution. It can be elegant and fun. Fall is chrysanthemum time, so they are the main theme for this buffet.

A white kimono with chrysanthemums, maples, streams and clouds in vermillion, navy blue and moss green, is hung on the wall, making a backdrop for an arrangement. Small, red, button chrysanthemums are arranged with white spider mums in a giant bamboo container resembling *Kakehi*, the bamboo water conduit used in Japanese gardens. Paralleling it, two more split bamboo containers are used on the table which is lined with a cinnabar-colored *obi* with a wild chrysanthemum design. The further one holds a colorful bouquet of black olives, carrots, cucumbers, yellow sweet peppers, boiled shrimp and boiled quail eggs, on bamboo skewers and stuck into daikon. The dipping sauces for the skewered food are in two lacquer soup bowls. Just in front of that, another bamboo container offers, from left to right, mixed rice crackers, *Kamaboko*, fishcake sandwiched with cheese and *shiso* leaves, yellow sweet pepper, *Kamaboko* sandwiches, and apple and persimmon slices. At the extreme left, a tray holds small pastries. The nearby red tray holds rolled sandwiches of smoked salmon and Chinese

99

Shao-mai dumplings.

In the center, a fan-shaped tray displays an edible picture similar to the design on the kimono! The base is slices of white bread cut into small sections to fit the tray, spread with cream cheese mixed with sour cream. The yellow cloud is made with sieved hard-boiled egg yolks mixed with mayonnaise, and the vermillion cloud is made with *Masago*, salted smelt roe. The tree is drawn with anchovy paste with stuffed olive flowers. Smoked salmon slices make lovely peony flowers nestled in the foliage of Italian parsley. Cucumber slices overlapping make the green fields. Finally, jewel-like salmon roe are sprinkled on the yellow cloud and on the white base, and some capers are sprinkled on the vermillion cloud to complete the colorful picture.

Even though it is all finger-food, a few dishes of blue and silver maples are provided. The napkins are made of traditional Japanese towels with *Kanoko* print. A black lacquer *Bonbori* style lamp stand adds elegance to the setting.

The punch is in an antique black lacquer bowl with a bamboo dipper, surrounded by small lacquer cups. Chrysanthemum flowers float in reminiscence of the old Chinese custom of drinking wine with floating chrysanthemums for eternal youth!

Takahashi residence
Berkeley, California

Rice Harvest

At the end of October or early November, new rice appears at markets. The freshly harvested rice has a subtle, unmistakable aroma and texture, making people eager for its arrival. In some areas in Japan, the rice straws are crafted into many objects.

Here, a pair of rice straw horses loaded with newly harvested rice stalks are trotting through the countryside, marked with a flowing line made with rice. On the orange sweep made with red lentils sits an old spool holding a bonfire of bittersweet vines.

The runner is made of warm, light-brown silk with a leaf resembling rice plant grass in white. Partially-glazed red clay ceramic dishes made by my late mother-in-law hold rice balls of new rice rolled with *Nori*, dry seaweed sheet. These are accompanied by a bit of pickled greens. Tea cups on black lacquer saucers are off-white porcelain with an equisetum design in black and gold. Beige napkins are folded like little wayside shrines decked with rice ears and are tucked into miniature backpack baskets. The chopstick rests are dried reed knots.

A galloping horse on the *Ema*, a votive tablet on the wall, is craning over to see what is happening!

Takahashi residence
Berkeley, California

Autumn Brown
with Evergreen Pines

Here is a very subdued table for the deepening fall season. The theme setter for this table is an old *obi* that belonged to my mother. The abstract pine design is woven in beige, gold, mustard, brown, green, light and dark blue, making a subtle but exquisite harmony. To emphasize the dark brown in the *obi*, I used these brownish-black rectangular plates which I made years ago in a ceramic class. Medium brown napkins folded into squares are placed on the dishes, each with a green maple leaf. On the right, a small brown tea pot with pine needles in white sits on a burnt cedar trivet. This is a special pot for steaming mushroom and clear soup. The top lid is a cup from which to drink the savory broth of the pot. It is a delicious and warming soup, very popular for fall. On the left is a miniature winnow basket with edible autumn foliage and nuts, potato chip ginkgo leaves, carrot maples, pine needles of fried noodles, roasted chestnuts and fried seaweed chestnut leaves. *Sake* cups sit on ginkgo leaves.

An aged piece of twisted wood, with four brown candles in screw-on candle holders, makes the centerpiece with bright green pine boughs.

Home of Mr. Rayer Toki
El Cerrito, California

105

Persimmon Sushi

Colored persimmon leaves are incredibly beautiful! Some are golden yellow, yellow with a greenish tinge, others are bright orange or orange with a green streak. Each one seems prettier than the last.

I have no heart to pluck green leaves from trees, but these fallen leaves are much too gorgeous to be left unused. So using them as wrappers for *sushi* is a great idea. They make a wonderful show on the table as you can see. Besides, they can be prepared ahead. They are pressed under a weight for two hours and they will be a conversation piece.

The big *sushi* barrel with the *sushi*, backed by an arrangement of drift wood and a persimmon branch with its fruit, is the main feature on this table. Leaf-shaped dishes, processed from real leaves, are for serving *sushi*. The small cinnabar-colored dishes are for soy sauce. Orange napkins are folded to look like persimmons, and the chopsticks are in brown envelops. Please have some *sushi* with *sake* or green tea!

Takahashi residence
Berkeley, California

Maple Splendor

Nature has a magical way of staging a grand finale with trees, presenting a kaleidoscope show before shedding leaves for winter!

The scenery of hills and trees with coloring maple on the 18th century Kano School screen continues onto the table here. Maple trees in color grow by a bamboo fence, scattering leaves on a stream! Is it like some Kabuki play backdrop? The antique hand lantern *Teshoku* with red-lacquer frame strengthens that feeling.

The maple theme is repeated in the white porcelain covered bowls with red maple leaves for custard soup. These are set off by the red lacquer, half-moon trays. *Sake* cups of classic style set on maple leaves also are red. The rest of the table accessories are brown, the color of the dried leaves. The leaf-shaped dishes are processed from real leaves. Chopstick rests are gourds which are always associated with *sake*, because they formerly were used as *sake* flasks. The napkins are rolled into a brown napkin-ring of cord.

Here is a table where we can enjoy the glorious maple colors with *sake*!

Takahashi residence
Berkeley, California

Winter

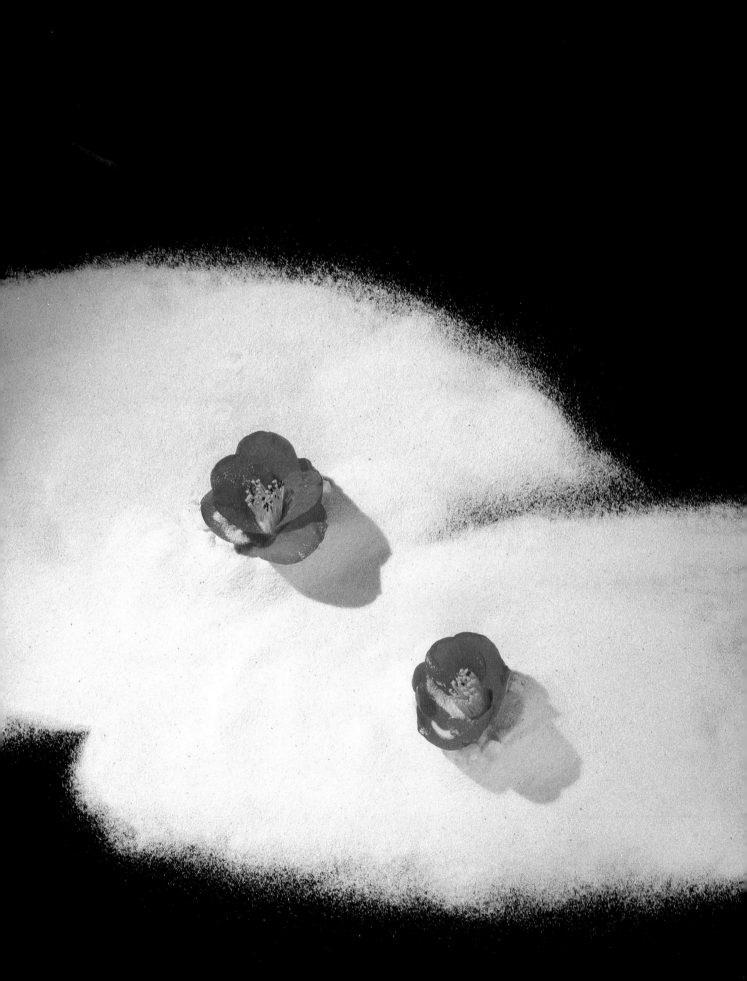

Gathering
of Kokeshi Dolls

A cozy winter lunch or supper becomes a festive table with a collection of *Kokeshi* dolls and carved wooden birds combined with candles. These folk toys were originally made by farmers during the long winters. Their simple designs, refined through generations, have a unique appeal. The red and white *Kasuri* woven cotton cloth in a traditional pattern makes a warm background for the natural tan of the wood, bamboo and the unglazed casseroles. The casseroles with a burnt straw design have a rustic charm. Served with red lacquered spoons, wouldn't they be great for a soup or stew? Woven bamboo trays are used as service plates and simply rolled red napkins repeat the cylindrical form of the *Kokeshi* dolls. The red sun in Masahiko Takata's *noren*, doorway curtain, shown here on the wall, relates to the round, red-lacquered bamboo dishes.

The *Kokeshi*, birds, *Kasuri* cloth, casseroles, bamboo trays, lacquer spoons and *noren*—everything is rooted in the traditional folk craft of Japan and results in a striking harmony!

Home of Mrs. Fay Kramer
San Francisco, California

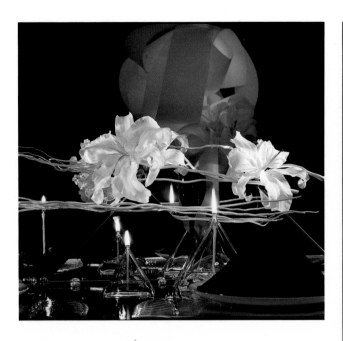

Black and White Fantasy

Nothing is more dramatic than the sharp contrast of black and white. Especially during the holiday season when bright colors are everywhere, severe black and white stand out as being extra chic!

Bleached willow branches and a cluster of majestic Casa Blanca lilies seem to be floating like clouds over several pyramids, which actually are triangular vases of mirror and black plastic. The triangular form is repeated by the oil lamps and the black napkins. Silver-rimmed white plates set off the black napkins and sit on silver plastic placemats of half-moon shape. The stemware is black glass. Glass marbles spread on the black table add glitter, reflecting light.

An apparition of lighted fiberglass work with white lilies, my ikebana sculpture, stands mysteriously in the back.

Takahashi residence
Berkeley, California

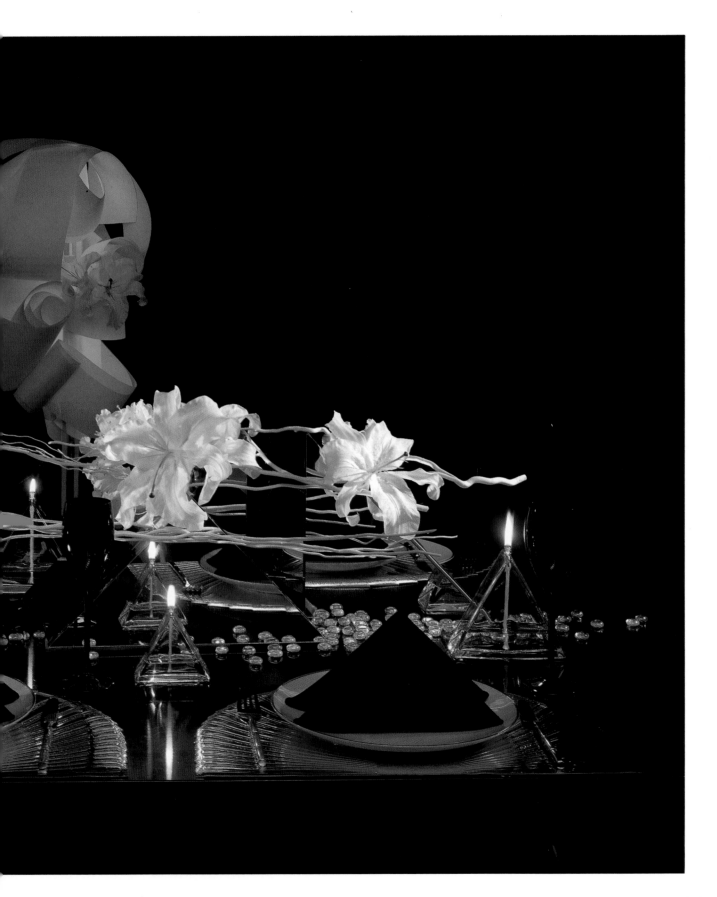

An Edible Ikebana

Store-bought snacks make entertaining easy. But they can also be elegant and amusing!

In front of this exquisite antique screen of bamboo, plum and camellia with snowy herons, a tree-like branch stuck with red cherry tomatoes mingles with the background, and adds a festive touch to this buffet. The branch is inserted into a heavy needlepoint holder on a black lacquer board. Twigs of parsley cover the holder, making a green mound studded with flowers of radish and green onion. A stream is shaped with flowing lines of salt. Several fish crackers swim in the stream and more fish are in a miniature fish basket. Peanuts form the river bar where cocktail sausages, cut in different heights, stand as river stakes. A bridge over the stream is lined with split sausages. Slices of salami sausage serve as garden stepping stones. A small stone lantern, black rocks, black pebbles and small bamboo baskets for the river embankment complete this miniature garden. Don't you think children would love to make this garden?

An antique lacquer rice bowl is used as a punch bowl, adding elegance suitable to this setting.

Home of Mr. & Mrs. Kent Atwater
Hillsborough, California

A Fireside Supper

During the busy social schedule of the holiday season, nothing is more relaxing than a quiet supper at home! With a bright fire in a fireplace, wine chilling in an ice bucket, hot soup and crusty bread on the table, nothing more is needed.

On this magnificent wall of natural field stone, early camellias and long lines of weeping willow arranged in a bronze moon container provide a seasonal touch of red. The color is repeated by the Japanese candle on an iron stand, and in the soup bowls, lacquer spoons, and the rolled napkins. Blue and red *Imari* plates set off the red lacquer soup bowls, and are placed on black, half-moon trays. The gold lacquer coffee table with matching cushions, has bamboo-shaped legs. Bread is in a smoked bamboo container and an antique *Hibachi*, a charcoal brazier, is used as an ice bucket.

Home of Mr. & Mrs. Martin Gordon
Corte Madera, California

Mexican Christmas

Christmas in Mexico is fun—full of color and joy which I wanted to reflect in this setting.

On the wall of this dining room a pastel painting in lavender, orange-red and shocking pink sets the mood for all the bright colors the Mexican artifacts bring in. A white Tree of Life has yellow, orange, red, green, blue, purple and pink, with purple candles. A donkey pinata is in red, orange and pink stripes. A German punch bowl and glasses sit on the Mexican napkins of mixed colors. Black candlesticks with red candles repeat colors in the framed picture, further echoed in the orange napkins in front of the Tree of Life.

A Danish table is set with a red runner with star embroidery in bright colors. Picking up colors from the embroidery, American yellow dishes are combined with Mexican blue cocktail glasses—perhaps for *seviche*? The bread plates are Japanese red lacquer and hold yellow napkins shaped into candles. The spoons and forks are placed face down, European style, as they are European antique and have a design and inscription on the back.

A translucent glass candle holder shaped like a large egg and filled with water is the centerpiece for this table, casting illusionary, refracted lights. The hollowed oranges with star shaped cutouts shed a warm glow with votive candles.

Terracotta figurines from Mexico: four carol singers and a grand dame decked with yellow mums and orange marigolds, all wish the diners, "Feliz Navidad!"

Home of Mr. & Mrs. Spence Sutherland
Sausalito, California

Christmas Magic

Sparkling lights on green wreaths twinkle like stars in the sky. Music and laughter from the living room fills the house. The table is surrounded by magnificently carved wooden chairs, and all is ready for a great Christmas dinner!

A wedding *obi* of Christmas red and green with gold on off-white makes a luxurious setting, flanked by bright red placemats. Brass candlesticks with metallic gold candles enhance the opulent feeling. A mass of green pine and holly branches is added, entwining the brass candlesticks. Since the design of the *obi* is cranes, several cranes in various sizes made with *Mizuhiki*, paper cord, are placed on the pine bough and on the *obi*. These cranes are the traditional ornaments for wedding gifts, and add an Oriental touch to the table, while tiny brass angels add that Christmas feeling.

Gold-rimmed, fluted, English plates not only repeat the crane wing design of the *obi*, but also repeat the gold and white tones, further emphasized by the gold-plated flatware. The red placemats set them off brilliantly, and they are balanced by the dark green napkins folded into *fleur de lis*. Name cards are tucked into the bottom fold.

Home of Mr. & Mrs. Iain Finnie
Berkeley, California

Reminiscence
of the Passing Year!

Just a few days are left on the old calendar! Under an old hanging scroll of Mt. Fuji in sumi-ink, an aged *tansu* which must have presided in a *Chanoma*, or family room, for several generations in Japan, is again witnessing another family gathering.

All the good omens for a prosperous New Year are here. On the *tansu*, a beckoning cat with a gold coin is smiling and a red lacquer candy box shaped like a sea bream, an auspicious fish, is flexing to jump. On the *Negoro* lacquer table—antique red lacquer with a black undertone—there are three good luck rakes with all the lucky ornaments.

A black square tray has delectable canapes of black and red caviar and cream cheese with an accent of black olives and capers. Black lacquer trays have pau-lownia family crests with a millet design in gold. *Imari* bowls hold rice crackers and nuts. Exquisite *Imari sake* cups surround a *sake* jug with *Sho-chiku-bai*, pine-bamboo-plum design, in blue. Red napkins with a small, white flower print are made from Japanese cotton towels.

Let us enjoy sipping *sake*, reminiscing about the past year, and talking about the coming year!

Home of Mr. & Mrs. Peter Sugawara
Los Altos, California

New Year Table
with a Bonsai

This California table expresses the serene, formal feeling of Japanese New Year with many auspicious omens. The *obi* runner is white with a gold hexagonal motif, signifying a turtle shell. As seen here a turtle is always paired with a crane for longevity. Cranes were said to live a thousand years, and turtles ten thousand years.

Intensifying the subtle gold in the *obi*, oblong gold placemats set off the white, fluted porcelain plates. Gold-plated flatware enhances the elegance. Rolled white napkins, tied with silver and gold *Mizuhiki* paper cord treasure-knots, are placed on the plates and add a formal note to the table.

The centerpiece is a magnificent bonsai of pine, plum and bamboo, the triple symbols of good fortune: pine for unchanging loyalty because it is ever-green; plum for courage and virtue for flowering in winter; and bamboo for resiliency. White and pink plum blossoms are so delicate against the ragged rock and aged pine tree. The black lacquer set of *sake* pitcher and cups are for *Toso*, an herbed *sake* served for New Year. The pitcher is decorated with *Noshi*, a folded paper ornament for ceremonial gifts.

Home of Mr. & Mrs. John Planting
Palo Alto, California

Coffee Break
During New Year

In a California living room with a redwood and flag stone wall, a rising sun scroll with gold mist and a verdant pine tree bonsai make a beautiful setting for New Year!

In front of the *Tokonoma*, a picture alcove, a coffee table is set to enjoy a cup of good coffee with baba au rhum. The table is lined with a gold *obi* with orange, wave-like lines running through it. Coffee is served in small *Oribe* cups on wooden saucers. The small babas are on fan-shaped bamboo dishes. Orange trays which intensify the color of the *obi* hold the cups and the dishes. On the table, a New Year touch is added by a small dancing doll. The doll, with its black lacquer hat with a red sun and a handbell, is dancing *Sanbanso*, a ritualistic dance for New Year.

Home of Mr. & Mrs. John Planting
Palo Alto, California

New Year Brilliance

Here is a table for a Japanese New Year feast. It is set in front of a magnificent screen of the Kano School, with a flowering plum tree by a stream, banked with camellias and peonies. The gold cloud seems to descend from the screen onto the table and to settle on the brilliant vermillion *obi* and on the red lacquer tray with food. For the individual settings, instead of more common lacquer trays, orange and white folded paper with pockets for chopsticks is used, setting off the black lacquer soup bowls and dishes. The gold crane motif on the soup bowls identifies them almost exclusively with New Year or weddings and are perfect with the gold cloud. Red napkins are also folded into the shape of cranes.

Young green pine is arranged with white camellia and circles of gold *Mizuhiki* paper cord, all in a black lacquer container with a gold cloud edge. A pair of antique lacquer candlesticks with Japanese candles and the exquisite stacked boxes seem to balance the predominant orange with the elegant black.

The orange lacquer tray holding food is made in a shape of *Hagoita*, a battledore, or racket used in a traditional New Year game. The tray is adorned with clouds and cranes in gold. The picturesque hors d'oeuvres are turnip chrysanthemums topped with red caviar, fried prawns, and crab meat rolled with egg sheet and *nori*.

Home of Mr. & Mrs. George Morishige
Berkeley, California

Welcoming
New Year Visitors

Here is a table to welcome visitors who may drop in for New Year greetings.

The wall is hung with an exquisite *Tsuzure*, a fingernail brocade with the rising sun and a flying crane over gold mist. An arrangement in front of it includes green pine, red ilex and white camellia in a ricestraw boat, signifying a treasure boat, another auspicious theme often used for New Year. The tablecloth is a cotton *Furoshiki*, a wrapping cloth, with a colorful crane spreading its wings. The red lacquerware, the tray, dishes and the *Toso* set make the table very festive, picking up the color of the sun, ilex and the crane's wing on the *furoshiki*. The foods on the red tray are small striped *sushi* of smoked salmon and cucumber, red plum flower canapes of smoked salmon with cream cheese, white plum flowers made with eggs, fried seaweed knots and gingko nuts pierced on pine needles. More food is stocked in the stacked boxes of black lacquer with a chrysanthemum design in gold. A small pail holds toothpicks. Napkins are *Kaishi*, bosom paper, with a family crest.

Home of the late Mrs. Harlan Taylor
Menlo Park, California

New Year Merriment

New Year is a festive time when children and grown-ups alike can indulge in playing games all day. Flying kites, playing *Hanetsuki*, hitting a shuttlecock with the decorated battledore, and numerous indoor games including many card games are popular. One of the oldest card games is *Hyakunin Isshu*, one hundred poems by one hundred poets. This must have been devised as a way to memorize these poems. After players are divided into two teams, a reader reads the first half of a poem. The teams then rush to be the first to find the card bearing the latter half of the poem. The dishes on the lacquer trays are made like these cards with poems. On the table there are other types of playing cards. The weeping willow branches pierce white and pink balls called *Mayu Dama*, silk cocoons, originally made with a wish for a good silk culture. These are a very popular New Year decoration. The double stack of round *Mochi*, pounded rice cake, is an offering every household will have, here topped with a fresh, leafy tangerine. The white mask *Otafuku*, a smiling, round-cheeked woman, is a symbol of good fortune and happiness. There is also a pair of smaller masks, one is *Otafuku* and the other is a tipsy buffoon. Some papier-mache New Year floats of red sea breams, with and without riders, join in as do a wooden toy horse and a lion dance. Resting next to *Otafuku*

137

is a ball of colorful, silken thread.

The black serving trays hold the card dishes and classical red *sake* cups. The chopstick rests are *Otafuku* masks. Red napkins are folded like *Noshi*, the folded paper decoration for formal gifts, enlivened with green bamboo leaves.

In the background hangs an exquisite screen of bamboo, plum and camellia, and a *Hagoita*, the decorated battledore with the face of a Kabuki lion dancer, is displayed. An antique lacquer candlestick and rice bowl on the brocade *obi* runner add a note of elegance to the festivity.

Home of Mr. & Mrs. Kent Atwater
Hillsborough, California

These are small dishes shaped and decorated like the cards used in the game "Hyakunin Isshu".

139

Authentic tea ceremony setting in the California home of Mr. & Mrs. George Morishige.

Chopstick holders come in many shapes to add a special touch to any table setting.

The Author and Production Team

Kuwako Takahashi formed a team of three longtime friends and colleagues to help bring her sketches to life and to photograph them.

Indispensable to the project was photographer Hugo Steccati. Meticulous, good humored, yet an absolute perfectionist, Mr. Steccati brought many years of experience as a successful commercial photographer to the project. He is a well known advertising and fine art commercial photographer based in San Francisco. Sally Sutherland helped with table setting and provided editorial consultation. Spence Sutherland was photographer's assistant to Mr. Steccati.

(Left to right: Hugo Steccati, Sally F. Sutherlland, Kuwako Takahashi and Spence Sutherland)

Have Fun with Napkins!

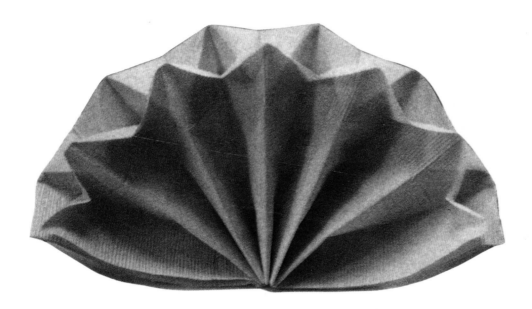

Kuwako Takahashi

Please note there are two kinds of folding line.

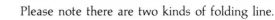

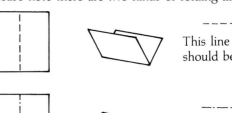

This line means the fold should be depressed.

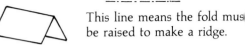

This line means the fold mus[t] be raised to make a ridge.

1. Love Knot (See pages 14, 15)

Fold in half diagonally.

Fold in from the long side.

1

2

3

4

A

Rolled up.

Fold B up first, then A over B.

B

Fold in two ends and make a knot by putting B into a loop.

5

B

A

6

7

Tuck in a branch of flowering plum.

2. Flat Helmet (See pages 42, 43)

1

8½″ (21.6cm)

10½″ (27cm)

2

A little off to the left.

3

Insert iris leaves.

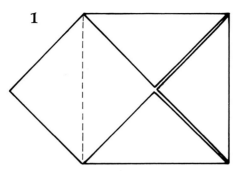

1 Fold all four corners in.

3. Lotus Flower

(See pages 46, 47, 56, 57)

4. Persimmon

(See pages 106, 107)

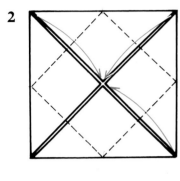

2 First folding.

Fold inside again.

3 Second folding done on the same side.

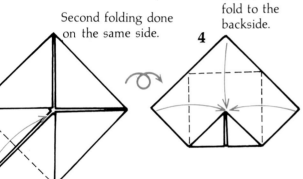

4 Turn over and fold to the backside.

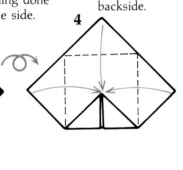

5 Third folding.

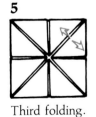

6

7 Holding the center with you right hand fold in each corner.

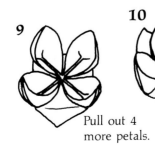

8 Pull out a petal from underneath.

9 Pull out 4 more petals.

10

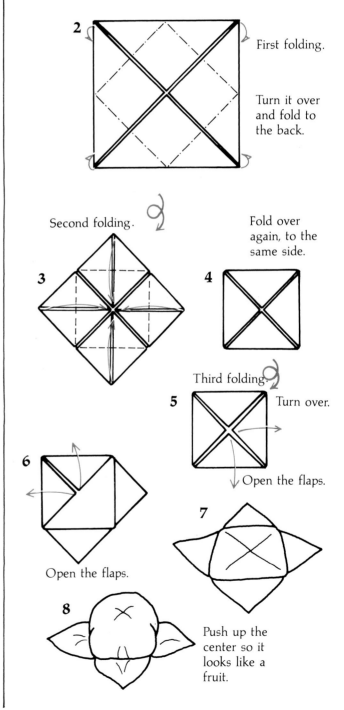

2 First folding.

Turn it over and fold to the back.

Second folding.

Fold over again, to the same side.

3

4

Third folding.

5 Turn over.

Open the flaps.

6

Open the flaps.

7 Push up the center so it looks like a fruit.

8

5. Goldfish (See pages 54, 55)

1

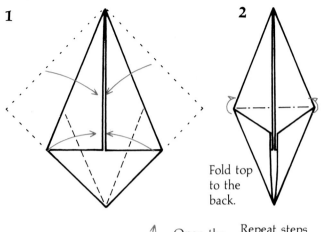

2

Fold top to the back.

4 Pull out.

Open the left flap.

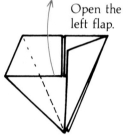

Repeat steps 3 & 4 on right hand side.

5

6

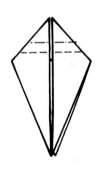

7

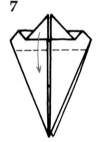

8

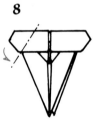

9

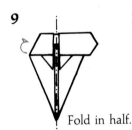

Fold in half.

10

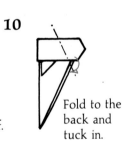

Fold to the back and tuck in.

11

12 Fold the tail between the front and the back.

Place the fish on a slightly concave dish, curving the body.

6. Rose (See pages 66, 67)

1

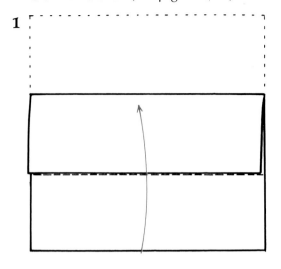

2

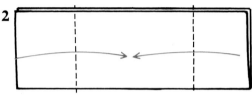

3

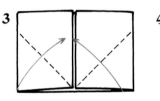

4 A B

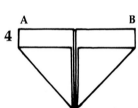

5 A B

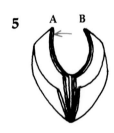

Holding the ends, bend away from you until ends meet.

Tuck B into A.

6

A B

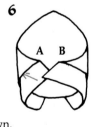

7

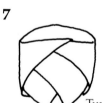

Turn upside down, and open up the petals.

8

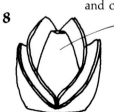

Push here with your finger to make the top face up.

7. Sunburst with a Back Support

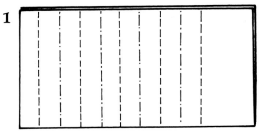

1

2

3″ (7.5 cm)

Make accordion pleats, but leave last 3″ (7.5 cm) unfolded.

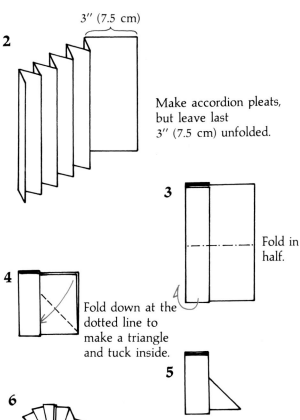

3

Fold in half.

4

Fold down at the dotted line to make a triangle and tuck inside.

5

6

Open the top.

This sunburst is more stable than the other one.

7

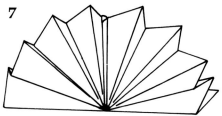

8. Sunburst (See pages 22, 23)

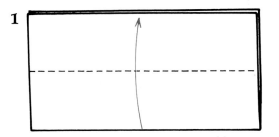

1

2

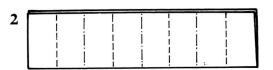

3

Fold down indented top between pleats.

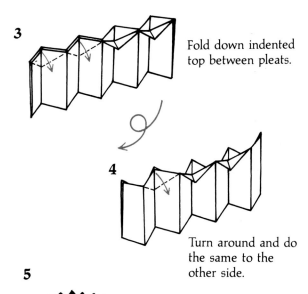

4

Turn around and do the same to the other side.

5

Press together lower side and open the top.

6

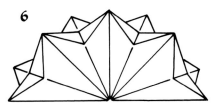

This is an example with minimum pleats. Increase the number of pleats for better result.

9. Double-decker Package

(See pages 50, 51)

A square sheet of medium weight paper, three times larger than the package (To make 7" (17.5cm) package you need 21" (52.5cm) square.) One sheet of this size makes a double-decker package. Use two sheets in harmonizing colors for dramatic effects.

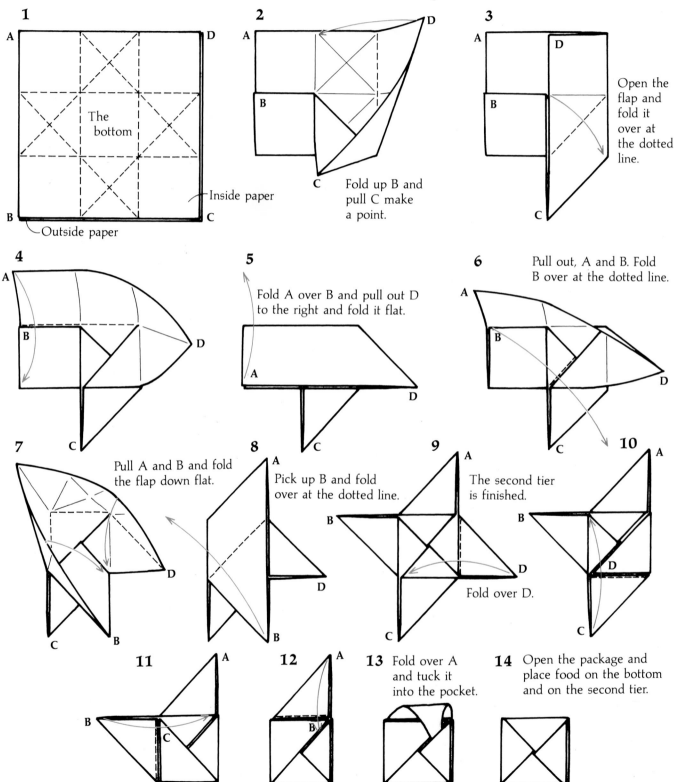

1 The bottom — Inside paper — Outside paper

2 Fold up B and pull C make a point.

3 Open the flap and fold it over at the dotted line.

4

5 Fold A over B and pull out D to the right and fold it flat.

6 Pull out, A and B. Fold B over at the dotted line.

7 Pull A and B and fold the flap down flat.

8 Pick up B and fold over at the dotted line.

9 The second tier is finished. Fold over D.

10

11

12

13 Fold over A and tuck it into the pocket.

14 Open the package and place food on the bottom and on the second tier.

10. Square Knot (See pages 104, 105)

1

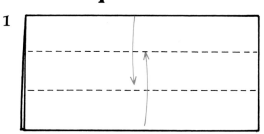

Fold on the dotted lines.

2

Fold ½″ (1cm) to the right of center.

B 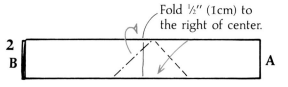 A

A end is folded down in front.
B end is folded back.

3

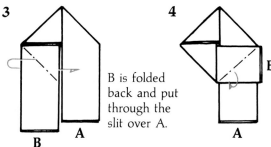

B is folded back and put through the slit over A.

4

B is folded behind and tucked under.

5

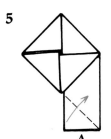

Tuck the end into the triangle.

6

7

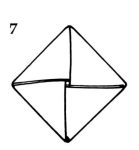

11. Hina Doll (See pages 26, 27)

1

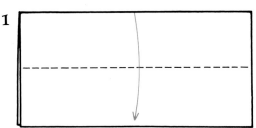

Fold in half and again fold in half.

2

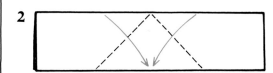

Fold both ends forward.

3

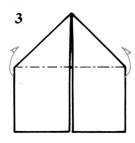

Fold back at the dotted line.

4

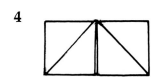

5

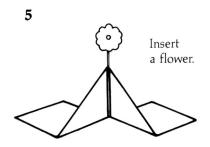

Insert a flower.

Name card.

Fan-shaped card may be pinned on.

151

12. Japanese Boat (See pages 68, 69)

1

2

3 Fold the ends to the center.

Fold the four corners to the center.

4 Turn and open the folded flap.

Fold to the back.

5 Pull out the two corners.

6 Fold the flap flat to make a boat shape. Repeat with the upper side.

7

8
C   D
E   F

9 Pull out C-D flap and E-F flap and then fold back G and H and flatten them.

Turn it over.

11
A
C   D
E   F
B

12
A
D   C
F   E
B

Fold C D E F towards the center.

10
A
H C D G
B

Holding the center firmly pull out A and B unfolding them all the way as shown in No.11.

13
A
D C
F E
B

Fold up at dotted line.

14
A
B
Fold the bottom B up.

15
Fold the bottom up again.

16

17 Fold in half lengthwise.
A
B

18
B   A
Pull out A and B and pull them upwards.

19

13. Bamboo Boat

1

2 Cut.
A
B

3
A
B

4
Put B through A loop.

152

14. Lily: Fleur de Lis (See pages 122–125)   15. Helmet

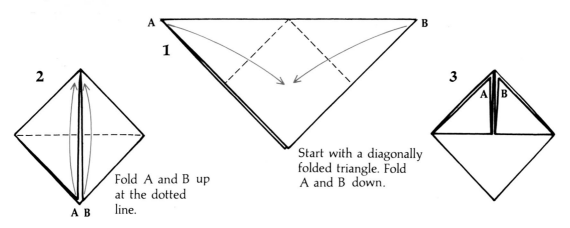

1 Start with a diagonally folded triangle. Fold A and B down.

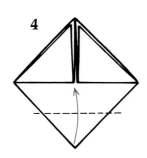

2 Fold A and B up at the dotted line.

3

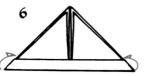

4

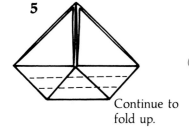

5 Continue to fold up.

6 Fold both ends away from you until they meet.

Backside.

7 Tuck one end into the other.

8

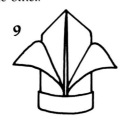

9

4

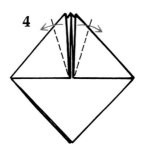

5

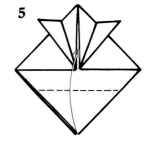

6

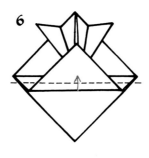

7 Fold to the back at the dotted line.

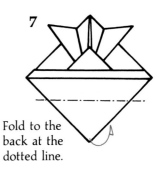

Backside.

8 Fold up.

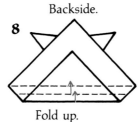

9

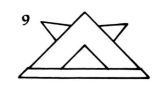

10 Make it stand by opening the base.

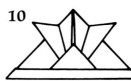

153

16. Cutlery Holder (See pages 62, 63)

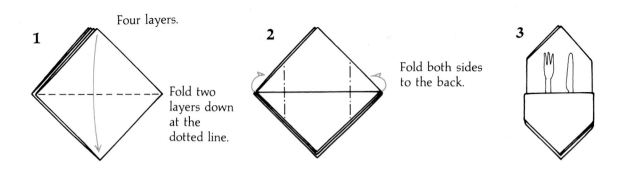

1 Four layers.

Fold two layers down at the dotted line.

2 Fold both sides to the back.

3

17. Folded Square (See pages 90, 91)

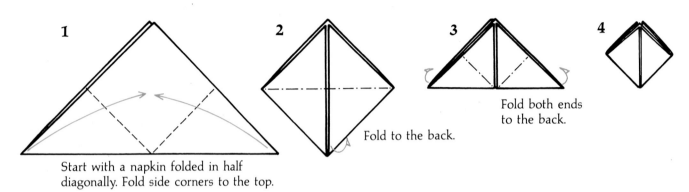

1 Start with a napkin folded in half diagonally. Fold side corners to the top.

2 Fold to the back.

3 Fold both ends to the back.

4

18. Witch Hat (See pages 92, 93)

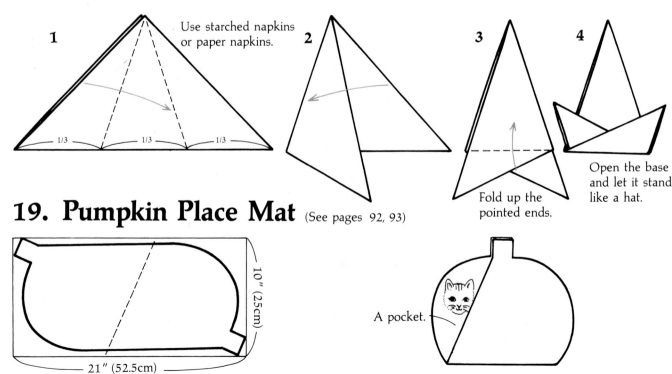

1 Use starched napkins or paper napkins.

1/3   1/3   1/3

2

3 Fold up the pointed ends.

4 Open the base and let it stand like a hat.

19. Pumpkin Place Mat (See pages 92, 93)

10" (25cm)

21" (52.5cm)

A pocket.

154

20. Crown

21. Open Pyramid

(See pages 114, 115)

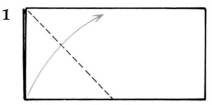

Start with a napkin folded in half.

Fold up the lower left corner to the center.

 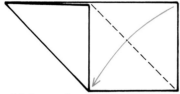

Fold down the upper right corner.

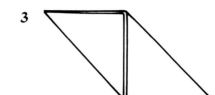

Fold in half.

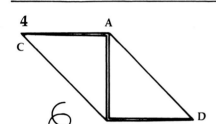

Fold forward at the dotted line.

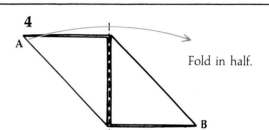

Fold A to the back.

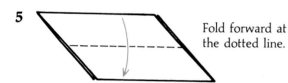

Fold C to the back and tuck the tip under B.

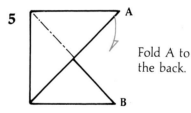

Fold B to the front.

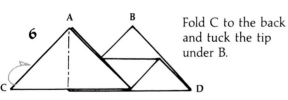

Fold D to the front and tuck the tip under A.

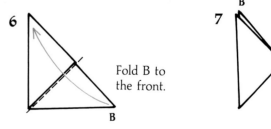

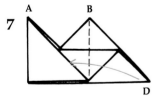

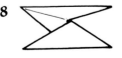

Birdseye view.

Open the base to stand.

Open and let it stand up.

155

22. Candle (See pages 120, 121)

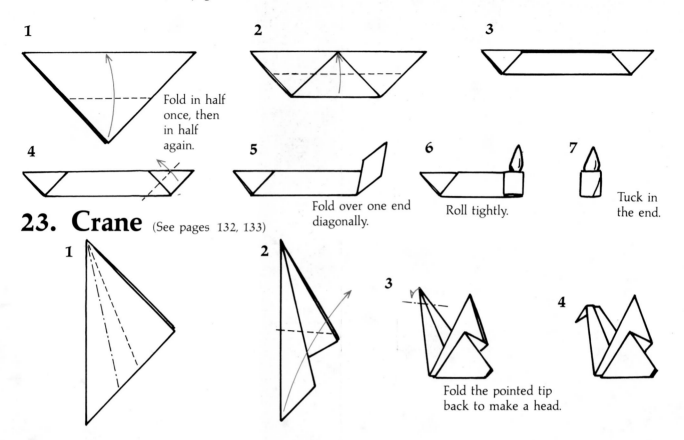

1

2

3

Fold in half once, then in half again.

4

5 Fold over one end diagonally.

6 Roll tightly.

7 Tuck in the end.

23. Crane (See pages 132, 133)

1

2

3 Fold the pointed tip back to make a head.

4

24. Place Mats (See pages 84, 85)

Buy 20" × 26" (50cm × 65cm) paper and cut in half.
Use two sheets for one mat, in contrasting colors.

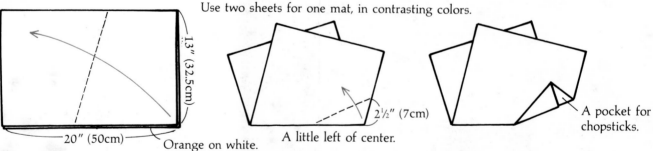

13" (32.5cm)

20" (50cm)

Orange on white.

2½" (7cm)

A little left of center.

A pocket for chopsticks.

25. Noshi, ceremonial gift ornament (See pages 136, 137)

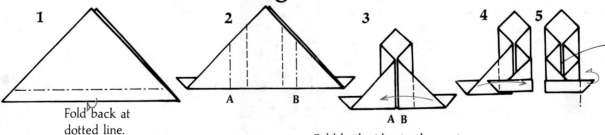

1 Fold back at dotted line.

2 A   B

3 A B
Fold both sides to the center putting A and B together.

4

5 Fold right tip under and insert a name card, a leaf, or a flower.